Francis Frith's
RINGWOOD

Photographic Memories

Francis Frith's

RINGWOOD

Mary Baldwin

FRITH
BOOK Co

First published in the United Kingdom in 2001 by
Frith Book Company Ltd

Paperback Edition 2001
ISBN 1-85937-384-4

Hardback Edition 2002
ISBN 1-85937-573-1

Reprinted in paperback 2002

British Library Cataloguing in Publication Data

Francis Frith's Ringwood
Mary Baldwin

Frith Book Company Ltd
Frith's Barn, Teffont,
Salisbury, Wiltshire SP3 5QP
Tel: +44 (0) 1722 716 376
Email: info@francisfrith.co.uk
www.francisfrith.co.uk

Printed and bound in Great Britain

Front Cover: Ringwood, High Street c1955 R35017

Contents

FRANCIS FRITH, Victorian founder of the world-famous photographic archive, was a devout Quaker and a highly successful Victorian businessman, philosophic by nature and pioneering in out-look.

By 1855 Francis Frith had already established a wholesale grocery business in Liverpool, and sold it for the astonishing sum of £200,000, which is the equivalent today of over £15,000,000. Now a multi-millionaire, he was able to indulge his passion for travel. As a child he had pored over travel books written by early explorers, and his fancy and imagination had been stirred by family holidays to the sublime mountain regions of Wales and Scotland. 'What a land of spirit-stirring and enriching scenes and places!' he had written. He was to return to these scenes of grandeur in later years to 'recapture the thousands of vivid and tender memories', but with a different purpose. Now in his thirties, and captivated by the new science of photography, Frith set out on a series of pioneering journeys to the Nile regions that occupied him from 1856 until 1860.

INTRIGUE AND ADVENTURE

He took with him on his travels a specially-designed wicker carriage that acted as both dark-room and sleeping chamber. These far-flung journeys were packed with intrigue and adventure. In his life story, written when he was sixty-three, Frith tells of being held captive by bandits, and of fighting 'an awful midnight battle to the very point of surrender with a deadly pack of hungry, wild dogs'. Sporting flowing Arab costume, Frith arrived at Akaba by camel seventy years before Lawrence, where he encountered 'desert princes and rival sheikhs, blazing with jewel-hilted swords'.

During these extraordinary adventures he was assiduously exploring the desert regions bordering the Nile and patiently recording the antiquities and peoples with his camera. He was the first photographer to venture beyond the sixth cataract. Africa was still the mysterious 'Dark Continent', and Stanley and Livingstone's historic meeting was a decade into the future. The conditions for picture taking confound belief. He laboured for hours in his wicker dark-room in the sweltering heat of the desert, while the volatile chemicals fizzed dangerously in their trays. Often he was forced to work in remote tombs and caves where conditions were cooler. Back in London he exhibited his photographs and was 'rapturously cheered' by members of the Royal Society. His reputation as a photographer was made overnight. An eminent modern historian has likened their impact on the population of the time to that on our own generation of the first photographs taken on the surface of the moon.

VENTURE OF A LIFE-TIME

Characteristically, Frith quickly spotted the opportunity to create a new business as a specialist publisher of photographs. He lived in an era of immense and sometimes violent change. For the poor in the early part of Victoria's reign work was a drudge and the hours long, and people had precious little free time to enjoy themselves. Most had no transport other than a cart or gig at their disposal, and had not travelled far beyond the boundaries of their own town or village.

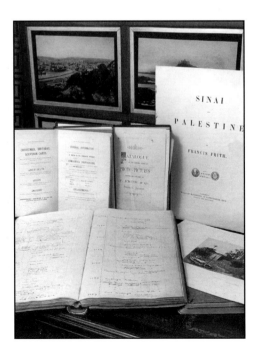

However, by the 1870s, the railways had threaded their way across the country, and Bank Holidays and half-day Saturdays had been made obligatory by Act of Parliament. All of a sudden the ordinary working man and his family were able to enjoy days out and see a little more of the world.

With characteristic business acumen, Francis Frith foresaw that these new tourists would enjoy having souvenirs to commemorate their days out. In 1860 he married Mary Ann Rosling and set out with the intention of photographing every city, town and village in Britain. For the next thirty years he travelled the country by train and by pony and trap, producing fine photographs of seaside resorts and beauty spots that were keenly bought by millions of Victorians. These prints were painstakingly pasted into family albums and pored over during the dark nights of winter, rekindling precious memories of summer excursions.

THE RISE OF FRITH & CO

Frith's studio was soon supplying retail shops all over the country. To meet the demand he gathered about him a small team of photographers, and published the work of independent artist-photographers of the calibre of Roger Fenton and Francis Bedford. In order to gain some understanding of the scale of Frith's business one only has to look at the catalogue issued by Frith & Co in 1886: it runs to some 670 pages, listing not only many thousands of views of the British Isles but

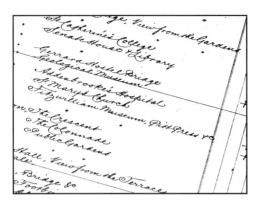

also many photographs of most European countries, and China, Japan, the USA and Canada – note the sample page shown above from the hand-written *Frith & Co* ledgers detailing pictures taken. By 1890 Frith had created the greatest specialist photographic publishing company in the world, with over 2,000 outlets – more than the combined number that Boots and W H Smith have today! The picture on the right shows the *Frith & Co* display board at Ingleton in the Yorkshire Dales. Beautifully constructed with mahogany frame and gilt inserts, it could display up to a dozen local scenes.

POSTCARD BONANZA

The ever-popular holiday postcard we know today took many years to develop. In 1870 the Post Office issued the first plain cards, with a pre-printed stamp on one face. In 1894 they allowed other publishers' cards to be sent through the mail with an attached adhesive halfpenny stamp. Demand grew rapidly, and in 1895 a new size of postcard was permitted called the court card, but there was little room for illustration. In 1899, a year after

Frith's death, a new card measuring 5.5 x 3.5 inches became the standard format, but it was not until 1902 that the divided back came into being, with address and message on one face and a full-size illustration on the other. *Frith & Co* were in the vanguard of postcard development, and Frith's sons Eustace and Cyril continued their father's monumental task, expanding the number of views offered to the public and recording more and more places in Britain, as the coasts and countryside were opened up to mass travel.

Francis Frith died in 1898 at his villa in Cannes, his great project still growing. The archive he created continued in business for another seventy years. By 1970 it contained over a third of a million pictures of 7,000 cities, towns and villages. The massive photographic record Frith has left to us stands as a living monument to a special and very remarkable man.

FRANCIS FRITH'S legacy to us today is of immense significance and value, for the magnificent archive of evocative photographs he created provides a unique record of change in 7,000 cities, towns and villages throughout Britain over a century and more. Frith and his fellow studio photographers revisited locations many times down the years to update their views, compiling for us an enthralling and colourful pageant of British life and character.

We tend to think of Frith's sepia views of Britain as nostalgic, for most of us use them to conjure up memories of places in our own lives with which we have family associations. It often makes us forget that to Francis Frith they were records of daily life as it was actually being lived in the cities, towns and villages of his day. The Victorian age was one of great and often bewildering change for ordinary people, and though the pictures evoke an impression of slower times, life was as busy and hectic as it is today. We are fortunate that Frith was a photographer of the people, dedicated to recording the minutiae of everyday life. For it is this sheer wealth of visual data, the painstaking chronicle of changes in dress, transport, street layouts, buildings, housing, engineering and landscape that captivates us so much today. His remarkable images offer us a powerful link with the past and with the lives of our ancestors.

TODAY'S TECHNOLOGY

Computers have now made it possible for Frith's many thousands of images to be accessed almost instantly. In the Frith archive today, each photograph is carefully 'digitised' then stored on a CD Rom. Frith archivists can locate a single photograph amongst thousands within seconds. Views can be catalogued and sorted under a variety of categories of place and content to the immediate benefit of researchers. Inexpensive reference prints can be created for them at the touch of a mouse button, and a wide range of books and other printed materials assembled and published for a wider, more general readership - in the next twelve months over a hundred Frith local history titles will be published! The day-to-day workings of the archive are very different from how they were in Francis Frith's time: imagine the herculean task of sorting through eleven tons of glass negatives as Frith had to do to locate a particular

See Frith at www.francisfrith.co.uk

sequence of pictures! Yet the archive still prides itself on maintaining the same high standards of excellence laid down by Francis Frith, including the painstaking cataloguing and indexing of every view.

It is curious to reflect on how the internet now allows researchers in America and elsewhere greater instant access to the archive than Frith himself ever enjoyed. Many thousands of individual views can be called up on screen within seconds on one of the Frith internet sites, enabling people living continents away to revisit the streets of their ancestral home town, or view places in Britain where they have enjoyed holidays. Many overseas researchers welcome the chance to view special theme selections, such as transport, sports, costume and ancient monuments.

We are certain that Francis Frith would have heartily approved of these modern developments, for he himself was always working at the very limits of Victorian photographic technology.

THE VALUE OF THE ARCHIVE TODAY

Because of the benefits brought by the computer, Frith's images are increasingly studied by social historians, by researchers into genealogy and ancestory, by architects, town planners, and by teachers and schoolchildren involved in local history projects. In addition, the archive offers every one of us a unique opportunity to examine the places where we and our families have lived and worked down the years. Immensely successful in Frith's own era, the archive is now, a century and more on, entering a new phase of popularity.

THE PAST IN TUNE WITH THE FUTURE

Historians consider the Francis Frith Collection to be of prime national importance. It is the only archive of its kind remaining in private ownership and has been valued at a million pounds. However, this figure is now rapidly increasing as digital technology enables more and more people around the world to enjoy its benefits.

Francis Frith's archive is now housed in an historic timber barn in the beautiful village of Teffont in Wiltshire. Its founder would not recognize the archive office as it is today. In place of the many thousands of dusty boxes containing glass plate negatives and an all-pervading odour of photographic chemicals, there are now ranks of computer screens. He would be amazed to watch his images travelling round the world at unimaginable speeds through network and internet lines.

The archive's future is both bright and exciting. Francis Frith, with his unshakeable belief in making photographs available to the greatest number of people, would undoubtedly approve of what is being done today with his lifetime's work. His photographs, depicting our shared past, are now bringing pleasure and enlightenment to millions around the world a century and more after his death.

The photographer for Frith & Co first set up his camera in Ringwood in the 1890s. According to Brabner's Gazeteer of 1895, Ringwood was then

'a town in Hampshire with a station on the London & South West Railway and a post and telegraph office. The town stands on the River Avon, at the junction of the railway to Christchurch, on the verge of the New Forest, 21 miles by road and 241/2 by railway south west of Southampton. It was long famous for good ale and for a particular kind of woollen glove; has still a brewery, some hosiery manufacture, and a large factory for agricultural implements. It consists chiefly of four streets diverging from a market-place, and has two banks, two chief inns, a large and handsome town-hall built in 1868, a lecture-hall, a theatre, a police station, three bridges, a public library with reading rooms, a church, an endowed school, almshouses, a workhouse, and charities. There are Wesleyan, Baptist, Unitarian and Congregational chapels. A weekly general market is held on Wednesday, a cattle market on every alternate Wednesday, and fairs on 10 July and 11 December.'

The four chief streets mentioned above form the framework of this book of Frith

Ringwood Church 1890 24064

photographs. Ringwood first grew up at the junction of these roads as they converged at a crossing point on the River Avon.

The town's inclusion in the Domesday Book of 1086 proves its origins date back to at least Saxon times. Its main function has always been as a trading centre for the surrounding area. Further to this it was a stopping place for travellers immediately before or after their long, and sometimes dangerous, journey across the New Forest. By the Middle Ages the town was the established market for the New Forest and an administrative centre of some importance. Its significance is demonstrated by the fact that when the Duke of Monmouth was captured on Horton Heath in 1685, it was to Ringwood that he was brought for interrogation. However, Ringwood, unlike its neighbours Christchurch and Lymington, never received borough status and therefore never had a Mayor and Corporation or its own Member of Parliament. It remained a manor held by a succession of Lords, none of whom lived in the town. The last owners of the Manor of Ringwood were the Morant family, who bought the manor in 1792.

During the 19th century, Ringwood's strategic point at the junction of the roads from London to Poole, and Salisbury to Christchurch, continued to maintain the town's reputation as a focus for trade. In 1847 the circuitous route of the Southampton to Dorchester Railway, nicknamed 'Castleman's Corkscrew', ensured that Ringwood was also included in the new railway system which transformed 19th-century transport. This helped to keep Ringwood 'on the map'. Nevertheless, as the new town of Bournemouth began its spectacular growth, so Ringwood's influence gradually declined. By the time the first Frith photographs were taken in 1890, Ringwood's heyday was already

The Town from Wimborne Road 1900 45029

Below: The River and Church c1950 R35021

There are various theories as to the origin of the name Ringwood. Some scholars suggest it derives from the Saxon 'Rimuc Wode' meaning the edge of the wood, but most seem to favour the Domesday version 'Rincvede', meaning a ford (vede) over a river (rine). This would be appropriate as Ringwood stands at a crossing point of the Hampshire Avon on the western edge of the New Forest. Here the river spreads out into several channels among low-lying meadows as it slowly meanders south to Christchurch.

Above: **Somerley House 1891** 28651

over, although the town remained - as over past centuries - characterised by a way of life largely based on local agriculture and its associated trades.

In 1890 the Lord of the Manor was John Morant Esquire, who owned many farms and properties in Ringwood: practically all of Poulner, several inns and shops, the Town Hall and the rights to the weekly market. Mr Morant lived at Brockenhurst Park in the New Forest and only visited Ringwood on special occasions, but his younger brother Hay Richards Morant lived in Ringwood Manor House and took a lively interest in the town. Other notable local landowners were the Earl of Normanton at Somerley Park and John Mills Esquire of Bisterne House. The population of the parish of Ringwood was then about 4000, comprising a social mixture ranging from those gentry living on private means to the inmates of Ringwood Workhouse who lived on the parish.

Over the past century, both the population and the road network have grown so much that parts of Ringwood have changed beyond recognition. Nevertheless, despite some unfortunate demolition, particularly in the 1960s, many of the buildings in the original streets featured in this Frith collection have survived.

Nowadays the heart of the old town is a designated Conservation Area, which the people of Ringwood regard as a valued part of their historic heritage.

Above: **Avon Castle 1891** 28650

Right: **Moyles Court 1891** 28654

Notable properties around Ringwood include Somerley House, the seat of the Earl of Normanton (see page 17), Avon Castle, built by John Turner-Turner in 1875, and Moyles Court, once the home of Dame Alice Lisle.

The Town from the River 1890 24052

A hundred years ago, anyone travelling on the main road eastwards from Wimborne or Poole would have passed through Ringwood over the three bridges that feature on the town's crest.

The First Bridge, otherwise known as Scutt's or Carter's Bridge, is the small single-arch brick bridge spanning the Millstream in West Street. The three-arched Second Bridge, which crosses the main river Avon, still stands next to the thatched Fish Inn. Known alternatively as Stoning, Old or Great Bridge, it has always been Ringwood's main bridge and has been rebuilt many times. The Third Bridge crossed the most westerly branch of the river (see 24052). It was demolished in the late 1960s when the main road was widened, about the time of the construction of the Spur Road to Bournemouth. Its older, alternative name of Treening Bridge comes from the Old English word meaning 'made of wood', although by the time of its demolition the bridge was a substantial four-arched bridge of stone.

The Millstream flows off the River Avon north of the church and meanders picturesquely along the southerly borders of the town by the open space known as the Bickerley. Its chief purpose in Saxon times was to provide power for the town's mill. The Norman Domesday Book of 1086 recorded that a church and a mill were by then already established in Ringwood, suggesting a pre-Conquest community of some consequence. The mill stood just north of the church on the narrow road to Fordingbridge. It occupied the same site for almost a thousand years, although the mill itself was rebuilt many times. The last mill to grind Ringwood's flour was erected in 1854.

The sites of both the mill and church are mentioned in the Ringwood entry in the Domesday Book of 1086. Ringwood miller's daughter, Mrs Helen Mary Slade (1903-2000), recorded on tape that during her Edwardian childhood at the millhouse, her father Harry Atkins employed a carter and his helper, four men in the mill and one boy.

The mill had been fitted with turbines and new roller-mill equipment made by J J Armfield Ltd of Ringwood, which produced whiter flour than the old mill-stones. The grist-mill, which was powered by its a separate water-wheel, still used two great mill-stones to grind animal feed. These stones had to be regularly dressed to keep their grooves deep enough. When they could no longer be used they were placed on the stable-yard floor. Four horses were kept to pull the wagon which delivered flour to Bournemouth and elsewhere, but this way of life ended forever after the First World War.

Opposite top: The Town fom The South 1900 45030

The number of small boats moored in many of the old photographs of the Millstream indicates that boating was more usual then than it is today. However, despite an attempt in the 17th century to make it navigable, the main Avon was never much used for transport. Fishing rights to the salmon and trout were considered paramount.

Opposite below: West Street c1950 R35031

Below: The Old Bridge c1950 R35030

The Hampshire Avon has always been noted for the quality of its fishing. Hunt's Directory of Hampshire (1852) states that 'many fine trout and some other fish are found in the rapid running waters of this rippling and translucent stream, which occasionally over-flows the adjacent meadows, and materially tends to increase the fertility of the land'.

The Mill and Church 1900 45031

At the time this Frith photograph was taken, the mill was owned by the Earl of Normanton and tenanted by the miller Mr Harry Atkins. After the First World War it was sold to the firm of J H Bartlett of Tisbury, who ran the mill until the 1930s. It was then demolished to make way for the first by-pass, which dramatically changed the way traffic travelled through Ringwood.

Above: The Millstream 1900 45032

The mill-house, which can be seen to the right of the mill, survived the first bypass and became known as the Avon Hotel, but this too fell victim to road improvement when the new bypass was constructed in the 1970s.

More than any other part of Ringwood featured in this collection, this area has changed out of all recognition over the past seventy years. If it were not for the existence of the parish church it would be very difficult for anyone from seventy years ago to get their bearings. The narrow Mill Lane leading from the Market Place towards Fordingbridge has disappeared completely. Where the actual mill stood is now under the tarmac of the A31. Today, only a few sluices remain of the site that for so many centuries had played such an important part in Ringwood's history.

Before the coming of this first by-pass, all travellers from the west, having crossed the Second Bridge, would have entered Ringwood via West Street, sometimes known as Bridge Street. A hundred years ago this was a picturesque road that became the favourite subject of many photographers.

Below: The Main By-Pass c1950 R35029

The car and lorry on this first bypass are passing over the approximate site where the mill and vicarage once stood. The narrow Mill Lane between the church and the mill has gone completely. In the 1950s traffic could turn into Ringwood at the junction by the Church, signposted the A338 to Christchurch.

The Millstream 1900 45027

This view shows a typical West Street scene of 1900. On the right can be seen the First Bridge spanning the Millstream with Carter's Brewery and Bridge House, the home of the family who owned the brewery, behind it.

In the earlier photograph (pages 28-29), the left-hand side of West Street is entirely lined by thatched cottages, with the notable exception of Monmouth House. The railings on which the man with the horse is sitting were erected in 1887 to mark Queen Victoria's Golden Jubilee. Ten years later the lime trees were planted to celebrate her Diamond Jubilee. These railings and limes originally extended all the way down the main Wimborne road to the Third Bridge, but nowadays only the ones in West Street remain. Before the trees grew up, the view from West Street back to the Fish Inn and the Second Bridge was much more open than it is today.

The Millstream was much wider and prone to flooding. These thatched cottages were very susceptible to flooding, with the waters sometimes reaching up to the Market Place. Since then the course of the Millstream has been altered, although the floods of November 2000 came close to the levels of earlier times. Many photographs in this collection clearly show the unmade gravel roads, which were muddy in winter and dusty in summer.

Ringwood has a long tradition of brewing and a reputation for good beer. In the 18th century there were malthouses and small commercial breweries all over the town. Carter's Brewery was the most famous, and the only one to survive into the 20th century. The brick three-storeyed Bridge House was built by Alexander Carter in about 1812. Next door was the Antelope Inn, which today forms part of Ringwood Social Club. Further up on the same side of West Street was another public house known as the New Inn, which was demolished about 1960. Carter's Brewery was bought out by Strong's of Romsey in 1923 and from then on there was no more beer brewed in

Above; **West Street 1900** 45026

Left: **The Old Cottages, West Street c1955** R35032

Ringwood until the present Ringwood Brewery was founded in 1978.

The tower of the Parish Church, topped with the Union flag, can be seen above the trees of the vicarage garden, which extended down to the Millstream. The vicarage stood immediately opposite the west end of the Church and was divided from it by a narrow lane. Its gardens were described as the most beautiful in Ringwood. They were swept away when the Vicarage, like the Mill, was demolished to make way for the first bypass. All that remains today is a small part that now forms the Jubilee Gardens.

The dilapidated thatched cottages by the river were converted into the Old Cottage Tea Rooms, now a restaurant. All the other thatched cottages were either pulled or burnt down and replaced by brick houses. After Carter's brewery closed, the site was used for the bus station and a row of shops. Bridge House became a hotel for many decades and is now the offices of Armfield Ltd. Despite the increase and noise of the passing traffic, West Street today is still a pleasant spot and a favourite with photographers.

West Street c1955 R35057

After the opening of the first bypass in the 1930s, West Street became quieter, as travellers passed by on the A31. Although it was still possible to travel up West Street, most traffic for Ringwood turned off by the Church.

Left: West Street c1960 R35119 **and detail above**

Monmouth House, with the white rendered front and gable, is noted as the place where the Duke of Monmouth, the eldest illegitimate son of Charles II, was held after the rebellion against his uncle James II failed in 1685. From here he was taken to London and executed on Tower Hill.

The Fish Inn from The Market Place 1890
24053

The three shops on the left were (from left to right) George Arney, saddler, Robert White, grocer and greengrocer, and Chissell & Co, butchers. Chissells later moved to the High Street. The building with the tall ladder against it was the New Inn. These buildings were all demolished c1960.

Passing up West Street, the road opens up into the wide Market Place. Dominating this area is the Parish Church of St Peter & St Paul. The church tower can be clearly viewed from every direction standing out above the town, as can be seen in many of these Frith photographs.

A church has stood in the Market place since Saxon times, although it has been rebuilt at least twice. The present building dates from 1853-55 and is a replica of the Early English cruciform church it replaced. The previous building had fallen into such a poor state of repair that the Victorians considered it preferable to rebuild it completely. Many of the original features of the earlier church were retained, including the medieval Purbeck marble shafts, some stone carved heads, the double piscina and the 15th century brass effigy of Dean John Prophete. White's Directory of 1878 describes the new church as 'a spacious and handsome structure with nearly 1600 sittings of which 766 are free. It has a large nave, chancel and transept, with a massive tower rising in the centre to the height of about 100 feet and containing eight bells.'

Above: The Church c1960 R35113

Left: The Church Nave East 1890 24065

The Parish Church is one of the best-loved and most used buildings in the town. This interior photograph, taken soon after the church was

rebuilt, shows that not a great deal has changed over the intervening years. The main differences are that the pulpit has now been moved further to the left so as not to obscure the chancel, and the wooden galleries above the side aisles have been taken down. Their removal in about 1922 allowed far more light into the building, but obviously decreased the seating capacity. Note the ornate brackets for the gas lamps which lit the church.

Below: The Cemetery 1890 24068

The new cemetery in Hightown Road was opened by the Bishop of Winchester in 1864, shortly after the Parish church was rebuilt. The two mortuary chapels were built of Swanage and Bath stone in the Gothic style, with a bell turret and centre spire 80 feet high. This photograph is taken from the cemetery looking south towards the road and the railway yard, now Castleman Way. The chapel on the left of the picture was for non-conformists, and the one on the right for Church of England use. Sadly, both chapels and their central spire were demolished in the late 1950s. They used to stand just inside the main gates on the area now used as a car park.

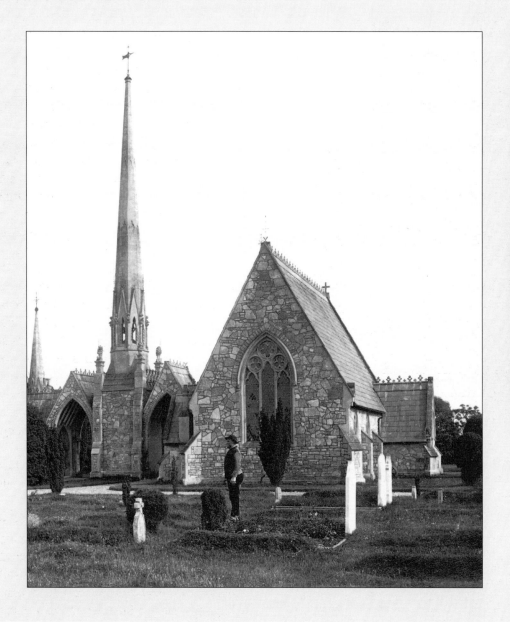

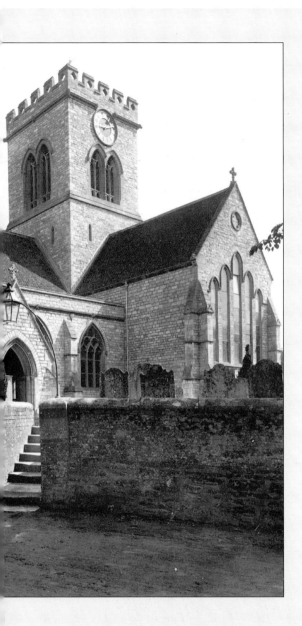

Above: The Church from South West 1890 24062

The steps in the centre of the churchyard wall were a useful way for the vicar and his parishioners to get straight to the church from the vicarage, immediately opposite the other side of the lane leading to Fordingbridge. Since the demolition of the vicarage in about 1931 the steps are now less frequently used, but they still remain as a way from the Market Place up to the churchyard.

The graveyard surrounding the present church is obviously far older than the church itself. The height of the graveyard above the Market Place below is an indication of how, over many centuries, successive burials have raised the ground level. Many thousands of bodies must have been interred here from Saxon times onwards, but we only know the names of these people since burial registers began in the 16th century. Very few legible gravestones survive from before the mid 18th century. Other than for a few exceptional interments, the churchyard was closed for burial when the new cemetery opened.

Outside the walls of the churchyard, the Market Place grew up as the commercial centre of the town, close to the church, mill and river. A Market Charter was first granted by Henry III to the Lord of the Manor of Ringwood in 1226. The rights to the Wednesday market are still retained by the last owners of the Manor of Ringwood, the Morant family. From its early days the Market Place gradually developed as a natural place for townsfolk both to live and work. Over the centuries permanent houses were gradually built, with some of the inhabitants using their front rooms to sell the wares they had made or bought. Many of the buildings in the Market Place have medieval origins, though all have been rebuilt at various times, mainly in the Georgian period. A century ago several of the properties in the Market Place were still occupied as private houses.

Few buildings in the Market Place have changed much over the last century, although the George Hotel and the Royal Oak were both completely re-fronted around 1900. Market places usually contain a large number of inns, which were used

Market Place 1890 24055

After the old Market House was taken down, it was partially re-erected on a new site at the beginning of the High Street (the steep-roofed building furthest from the photographer in this view). The building seen to its immediate right was a fine 18th century house, which during Victorian times was the home of the Dyer family. Thomas Dyer and his two sons Samuel and Henry all served Ringwood as doctors throughout the 19th century. It was Dr Samuel Dyer who tended the little boy injured in the accident in 1862 (see page 42).

The Jubilee Lamp, which stands in the middle of the Market Square, was erected by public subscription to

mark the Golden Jubilee of Queen Victoria in 1887. Here, the lamp is in original condition with five gas lanterns. On the central column was a drinking fountain with four spouts, from which water could be collected in four cast iron cups on chains.

not only for refreshment, but also for conducting business and for storage in their yards. Of the six inns or public houses in the Market Place in 1900, only three remain: the Original White Hart, the Star and the Red Lion (now Finn M'Couls). The White Lion closed many years ago and is now Scoltocks health food shop, the George has been recently converted into two shops and the Royal Oak is now a Chinese restaurant.

The early photographs give an impression of a much wider open space than today, now that car parking and an enhancement scheme have narrowed the expanse of road. On Wednesday market days there would have been a scene of hustle and bustle as farmers jostled to bid for animals, examine corn samples and exchange the latest news. At other times the street would have appeared very quiet by modern standards, with only the occasional cart or carriage passing by – though people at the time may have thought differently. In 1862 a correspondent to the Salisbury & Winchester Journal complained after a boy had been run over by a cart in the Market Place, 'What a number of boys congregate in our streets in the evening, particularly on market nights, when so many reckless Johns are driving through our town at a fearful rate, imperilling the lives and safety of the public with impunity'. Nothing is new!

Efforts to improve the town and ease traffic flow are also not a new idea. At the beginning of the 19th century there used to be a line of two shops and a Market House in the middle of the square. The Market House was an 18th century building with an open arched area underneath for market use and a room above for meetings of the manorial court. It was sited just east of the George Inn (approximately where the cart is standing in photograph 24055, pages 40-41). In 1808 the shops were demolished, and finally in 1867 the Market

Above: Market Place c1950 R35059 with details below

Left: Detail from R35059 showing Jubilee Lamp

By now, the appearance of the Jubilee Lamp has sadly deteriorated. The gas lanterns have been replaced by a single electric fitting, the drinking trough filled with concrete, and the column festooned with a collection of signs, including (by the 1960s) one pointing to the public conveniences.

The lamp was restored back to its original appearance to mark Queen Elizabeth II's Silver Jubilee in 1977. During the replacement of its stone plinth as part of the enhancement scheme in 1994, the base of the lamp column was uncovered, revealing it to have been cast by G Smith of Glasgow. At the same time the parking of cars and the snack bar, which had become a feature of this area, was no longer permitted.

House itself was taken down in order to open up the market area. It was partially re-erected at the beginning of the High Street, now the premises of Melson Wingate. Having cleared the old Market House, Mr John Morant, as Lord of the Manor, then built a new Town Hall and Corn Exchange next to the White Hart. It was opened with great ceremony in 1868, at a time when grand Town Halls were replacing older Tudor or Georgian market halls all over the country.

This was the time when Ringwood Market was in its heyday. Writing in 'The Ringwood Almanac' of 1903, an old resident of Ringwood recalled that when he was a boy, back in the

The Market Square c1950 R35026

early 19th century, Ringwood was a much busier place than it was by the turn of the 20th century. 'The great market-place nearly every week was full of cattle of all kinds. Cows, calves, horses, Forest Ponies, pigs etc were on sale, and cattle jobbers came to the markets from every direction, whilst on the pavement in front of the White Hart, the Red Lion and the George, farmers, dairymen and others met millers, corn and seed merchants, maltsters, nurserymen, dealers in artificial manures, sea-borne coals and other commodities, who regularly stood the market. But the scene is now changed, and what is left is but a fragment of the markets of olden times.'

Above: Market Place c1960 R35137

This view from the Market Place back to West Street shows (from left to right) the Red Lion Hotel, Baker & Son men's outfitters with a carnival display above, Pilley's tea-rooms, and St Mary's Fish and Chip shop. The buildings shown in earlier images (see 24053, pages 34-35) were demolished about 1960 and replaced by a nondescript flat-roofed block containing Barclays Bank and three shops with offices above.

Left: Market Place 1900 45036 **and detail right**

The building on the extreme right is Ringwood Town Hall, built by Mr John Morant in 1868. Next to it is the Original White Hart, unaltered from its appearance today, except for its lack of signs and the iron canopy over the doorway. As one of the two chief coaching inns of Ringwood, parts of the building possibly date back to the 15th century. It was re-fronted in Georgian times and again in 1868, the date above its doorway. To the left of the White Hart are the columns of the Victorian shop front of Cox & Hicks, drapers (see detail right).

In the late 19th century arable farming suffered an economic slump, so the Corn Exchange, as such, was never a great success. Nevertheless, it was well-used for balls, plays, concerts and indoor games. The Town Hall also contained a room for the court of local magistrates, and another two general-purpose rooms. In 1916 the Morant family were forced to sell almost all their estate in Ringwood, including the Town Hall. Following the break-up of the Morant estate, the Town Hall became the Victoria picture-house. In 1937 its frontage was drastically remodelled into the Regal Cinema, which was a popular place of entertainment for over three decades. It was also the venue for the productions of the Ringwood Musical & Dramatic Society until the cinema finally closed about 1970. Having gone through a period as a shopping arcade, this building has recently been used as a night-club.

On the retailing side, the Market Place has a long tradition of drapers and outfitters. Fifty years ago there were Cox & Hicks, W Ayles & Son, and F A Habbin, but today there is only Habbin's outfitters left. This shop now has the honour of being the only shop to still carry out the same trade, on the same site in the Market Place, as it did in the early 19th century.

By the 1950s the Town Hall (on the right in photograph R35025) has become the Regal cinema. Opposite it, the Dyer family's house was completely re-fronted in 1929 as the garage of E W Davis & Sons, with its pavement-side petrol pumps (now Wilds Sports). Note the distinctive copper beech and the chestnut trees standing near Letcher & Son solicitors, in the centre of this picture.

The building on the left in photograph R35060 was originally the Crown Inn in the 18th century, yet the front part became a bank during most of the following century. During the early

Above: Market Place
c1950 R35025

Left: Market Place
c1950 R35060

1900s it became used as the local council offices. At this time, it was occupied by the Ringwood Wholesale Company, but shortly afterwards it became Ormiston, Knight & Payne's estate agency, and its railings and the glazing bars of the ground floor windows were removed. The building has recently been restored and converted into private accommodation, now known as Old Bank House.

An unusual feature of the clothing industry in Ringwood, which flourished well into the 20th century, was the production of hand-knitted gloves known as 'Ringwoods'. The gloves were knitted by local women in their own homes in a distinctive 'Ringwood' pattern; two rounds plain, one round rib. This cottage industry can be traced back at least as far as the 18th century. The firm of Cox & Hicks, drapers in the Market Place for two hundred years, was closely involved in the collection and sale of the gloves. An inventory of their stock dated 1814 lists dozens of pairs of woollen 'knit gloves'.

During the 20th century the industry was revived by the firm of W Ayles & Son, who opened an outfitter's business in the Market Place in 1927. Mr Howard Ayles bought American cotton in bulk in fourteen different colours, and at one time employed nearly 900 women knitting the gloves for sale to the London West End stores. Yellow cotton gloves were particularly popular with horse-riders. Commercial production ceased about 1960, when competition from cheap machine-made gloves from the Far East made the hand knitting of gloves no longer viable. Nowadays it is not only Ringwood gloves that cannot be purchased; since the closure of Cox & Hicks in 1989, the only time a shopper can buy cloth or wool in the Market Place is on market day.

Traffic problems have beset Ringwood throughout the 20th century. The continued

Above: Market Place c1950 R35038 and detail left

A queue of people waits for the bus outside the George Hotel. Note the sign for the Riding Stables and the lamp over Rose's iron-mongers (see left). This shop, with its genuine Georgian double bow windows, was an iron-monger's shop for at least two hundred years.

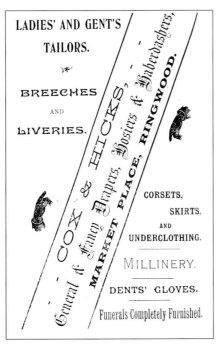

LADIES' AND GENT'S TAILORS.

BREECHES AND LIVERIES.

CORSETS, SKIRTS, AND UNDERCLOTHING.

MILLINERY.

DENTS' GLOVES.

Funerals Completely Furnished.

COX & HICKS,
General & Fancy Drapers, Hosiers & Haberdashers,
MARKET PLACE, RINGWOOD.

H. ROSE,

GENERAL AND FURNISHING IRONMONGER,

Stove & Range Fitter,

PLUMBER,

Gas and Water Fitter,

GUNSMITH, BELLHANGER, AND

AGRICULTURAL IMPLEMENT AGENT,

MARKET PLACE,

RINGWOOD.

SUN FIRE & LIFE OFFICE.
OCEAN ACCIDENT & GUARANTEE OFFICE.

Agent for Norrington's Manures.

congestion of cars and buses, despite the first bypass, necessitated the construction of a new bypass in the 1970s, which had serious implications for the Market Place. The point of entry for traffic into Ringwood was drastically altered, with the junction near the church being sealed off from the A31 by a brick wall.

Following this, the Market Place was no longer the entrance to Ringwood or its obvious centre. Although still acknowledged as the heart of the historic old town, the Market Place at the turn of the 21st century has had to adapt to this shift of focus.

Above: **Market Place c1960** R35138 **and detail right**

By 1953 the ironmongers had become Rose & Alexander (see enlargement right), after its new owners combined it with another branch in Fordingbridge. During opening hours the shop often had a collection of garden spades and forks on display outside the frontage, and an assortment of mowers, hose and tubs on the cobbles next to the pavement. Inside, the customer was greeted by the powerful smell of a glorious mixture of paraffin, sawdust and fertiliser. Next door, the courtyard under the archway of the Red Lion once had a cage containing a monkey, which fascinated many Ringwood children.

Right: **Market Place c1960** R35136

The private house for sale on the right of this photograph was the only building in the Market Place to be totally demolished in the 20th century. Around 1962 it was replaced by Ringwood's first purpose-built supermarket (now Keskins and the Imperial Cancer shop). With hindsight, this was a great loss for the Market Place as the supermarket soon outgrew this site, leaving behind a modern building of poor quality. During the 1960s there was a general move towards modernisation of shop fronts, in many cases not for the better. For example, Cox & Hicks drapers on the extreme left gained a modernised frontage in 1960.

Above: Market Place c1960
R35111with detail right

Judging by the decorations, this photograph of the north side of the Market Place was taken during September Carnival week. The gunsmith's shop is still trading, though its ownership has changed and the stock has diversified to include country clothing. Ringwood also retains a number of other traditional country sports shops, including a saddler and two fishing tackle suppliers.

Far Right: Market Place c1950 R35061

High Street c1950 R35039

Frampton & Son has the distinction of being Ringwood's oldest established business, although the shop is no longer owned by the Frampton family. A Charles Frampton was listed as a baker and grocer in the Ringwood entry in Sadler's Hampshire Directory of 1784. His grandson, Robert, was shown in the 1841 census as a grocer in the Market Place. His shop was demolished to make room for Mr Morant's new Town Hall. By 1871 Robert's son, Charles, had a small grocer's shop in the High Street,

next to their present shop, which was built in 1905. For many years in the first half of the 20th century, two of Charles Frampton's sons ran a grocery and corn-merchants business in partnership - Harry Frampton in charge of the grocery shop in the High Street, and Bill Frampton running the corn and seed business at Frampton's Yard. A third brother, George, owned the drapers in the High Street, which later became Guard's.

At the end of the Market Place the road narrows into the High Street, the traditional place for much of the town's shopping activity. The photographs from the Frith collection all show the High Street in the 1950s and 60s, a period of fond memories for many lifelong residents of Ringwood. Today the street still contains some of Ringwood's best-known local names, such as Frampton & Sons the seed-merchants and W Patterson the butchers, but many others have now gone.

A notable loss from the street scene today is the number of small independent grocers that used to supply the residents of Ringwood. By the 1960s the town had gained several supermarkets (International Stores, Pricerite and Keymarkets) but old-established firms such as Frampton & Sons still served groceries to their customers from behind an old-fashioned counter. Today Framptons has entirely dropped its grocery side in favour of the seed and garden supplies side of its business. All other independent grocers, such as Waller & Co and Charters, have disappeared. With them has gone that evocative smell of ground coffee, biscuits, spices and countless other mixtures that greeted customers as they entered the door to the familiar ding of the shop's bell.

Before the arrival of the supermarkets and multiples, most shops in Ringwood were run by families who had lived there for decades, if not centuries. Some owned their freehold and lived 'over the shop' for generations, but a surprising number of businesses changed premises within the town. Many businesses have had at least two different addresses over the years. Quite often the shop name changed as a former apprentice took over from his master or a married daughter and her husband inherited her family's business. Today the longest-established shop in town, still owned and run by the same family whose name is on the board over the door, is W Patterson, butcher, established in 1903, though not at its present site in the High Street.

Another familiar High Street name was once Brown & Son newsagents, stationers and printers. From 1901 to 1956 Mr Charles Norman Brown published an annual almanac which contained a most useful list of names and addresses of Ringwood residents and included advertisements for many leading businesses. Brown's Ringwood

High Street c1950 R35024

Inside Brown & Son, newsagents and printers, shown on the left, was a wonderful assortment of books, toys, china souvenirs and - of course - Frith photographs! Next door the Misses Bartlett sold cigarettes and sweets. On the opposite side of the road, Guard's drapers and outfitters was perhaps the nearest Ringwood came to having a department store.

Almanac and Directory of 1952, the year that Queen Elizabeth II came to the throne, records many of the familiar names of High Street businesses now closed. Names still well remembered included W A Ghrimes, furnishers and upholsterers, E W Pennell, tobacconist, W R Palmer, jeweller, and F Godden & Son, butchers. The name of Brown & Son itself disappeared from the High Street when the shop at Seldown House was sold to W H Smith in 1958.

The owners of many of these family businesses were often involved in many other sections of the community, standing as local councillors and acting on voluntary committees for local charities. This contrasts with some shop managers today, who may live elsewhere and be unfamiliar with the lives of their customers.

The same applied to the banks, where managers were also expected to be involved in

High Street c1950 R35052

On the left is E E Bickham's bakery. Today this shop has the distinction of being the oldest in the High Street to still carry out the same trade from the same premises. Though

the ownership has changed many times, a bakery has been here for at least 160 years and probably much longer.

Throughout the 19th century, censuses show the shop was run by a family named Ward. Early in the 20th century it was taken over by the Misses Cruttenden, three spinster ladies remembered for their delicious ginger-snaps. After them came Miss Mary Pennell and Miss Maggie Long, until the shop was acquired by Mr Eric Bickham.

Left: High Street c1960 R35134 **and detail below**

The distinctive hanging sign advertising teas and luncheons still exists, though it has been moved to the side of the building, facing onto Pedlars Walk, and now advertises coffee sold in the cafe above the bakery.

Left: High Street c1960 R35131

Barnwell's florist and fruit shop, on the right, was the only property with a thatched roof and a wooden shuttered bow window in the High Street during the 20th century. Both were then very unusual but would probably have been quite common a hundred years earlier. The shop was demolished about 1982 but its style was copied when the site was rebuilt.

the community. At the beginning of the 20th century Ringwood had two banks: the National Provincial and the Wilts & Dorset, both situated in the High Street. Only the former, now the National Westminster, stands on the same site a hundred years on. The London, City & Midland Bank (now HSBC) arrived in Ringwood in 1921, taking over premises previously used as a Coffee Tavern and Temperance Hotel and, before that, the Kings Arms public house. About the same time Lloyds bank (now Lloyds TSB) took over the Wilts & Dorset and erected a new mock-Tudor building on the other corner of Kings Arms Lane. Barclays bank only moved to the High Street comparatively recently; its first premises in the 1960s were in West Street. Today there are also four building societies in the High Street and another in the Market Place.

Fifty years ago very few women had their own cars, so almost all their shopping would have been done locally. This may have been supplemented by a day out on the bus or train to Bournemouth or Southampton to visit a department store or fashion chain. Eating out was then far less usual than it is today. Whilst there were several cafes in the High Street, such as the Old Brown House and Bickhams, restaurants serving foreign food and take-aways were unknown. One of the most noticeable changes between then and now are the number of Italian, Indian and Chinese restaurants in Ringwood today. Another change has been the arrival of many different charity shops. New technology and increased spending power have also brought changes to the High Street of the 21st century. However, despite the changes of owners and trades, the High Street of today is still easily recognisable in these photographs of between forty and fifty years ago, which will bring back happy memories to many.

High Street c1950 R35041

The south side of the High Street looked much the same as today. E E Topp, butcher, on the left of the picture, occupied premises that had been a butchers since early Victorian days. Previously it had been Chissell & Son, after their move from the Market Place. The rounded archway led to the back yard. Note the striped pole of Alfie Reynolds the barber, making his shop easy to find by anyone looking for a haircut.

Above: High Street c1950 R35017 with full image opposite below right
Opposite top: High Street c1960 R35129 with full image opposite below far right

These two photographs demonstrate the changing face of the High Street as shop fronts were modernised in the 1960s. On the left, in the 1950s picture (R35017), is traditional ironmongers E Chilvers. The premises of Watts & Faulkner, electrical suppliers, previously Mr Gadsby the photographer, are to the right. This was a good example of an 18th century house adapted in Victorian times by the addition of a small shop front.

In the 1960s photograph (R35129), Chilvers has been boarded up in preparation for a new frontage, (later Abbey National). Next door, the entire ground floor has been opened up for the new frontage of Fox & Sons estate agency (now a café), an action that completely changed the character and scale of the building.

Fridays Cross c1950
R35023

Miss Hardcastle, in her book 'Records of Burley', mentions a map of Burley of about 1700, which marked an orchard 'with the cross in it called Friday's'. Miss Hardcastle thought that this could refer to an old preaching cross, removed from its rightful place in Ringwood and planted in the Burley orchard after the Reformation. No trace of this cross now exists, so this must remain conjecture.

Arriving at Fridays Cross, the narrow road widens out again at its junction with Southampton Road and Christchurch Road. Nobody has come up with a definitive derivation of the name Fridays Cross. It goes back centuries and could be a corruption of a word or name now long forgotten. There is no factual evidence to suggest that anything of any historical significance ever took place here on a Friday. Whether there was ever an actual cross is also uncertain. Others believe the name Fridays Cross merely derives from the fact that this is where High Street, Southampton Road and Christchurch Road meet.

Papers in the Hampshire Record Office (11M61/56-60) show that there once were some buildings in the middle of Fridays Cross which were pulled down in the late 18th century in an attempt to improve the carriageway. Later obstacles in the middle of the road were a weighbridge and lamp-post, which were removed in about 1925. The road then became an expanse of tarmac (see R35130), until the Hampshire County Council enhancement of the High Street in 1993 narrowed the junction and added a circular metal seat.

To the right of Aldersons in R35130 is Hext jewellers. The Hext family came from Christchurch, where they had a watchmakers shop, in about 1870. The clock above their door, now so much part of Fridays Cross, was probably put up by Mr George Hext in the 1880s. Previously this shop had belonged to a watchmaker named James Adams who was also one of Ringwood's earliest photographers. Next to the Crown Inn is the dyer and cleaners, where Tommy Picton was usually seen hovering over his hissing steam press. On the far right is Sid Deedman's shop, from where many a small boy hoped he would receive a bicycle or model aeroplane for Christmas.

FAMILY   COMMERCIAL

AND   HOTEL.

F. PALMER,
CROWN HOTEL
Ringwood, Hants.

This Hotel offers capital ACCOMMODATION for GENTLEMEN and FAMILIES desirous of visiting this delightful neighbourhood, which embraces some of the finest Fishing on the Avon.

Conveyances meet all Trains at Ringwood Railway Station.

CARRIAGES TO ORDER.   LIVERY STABLES.

Ales, Stout, Wines and Spirits of the first quality.

Above: **Advertisement for the Crown Hotel**

Opposite above: **The Crown Hotel c1960**
R35130

Opposite below: **Southampton Road c1950**
R35040

Southampton Road c1960
R35128

Dominating Fridays Cross is the Crown Hotel. Originally named the Kings Head, its name was changed to the Crown about 1801. Along with the White Hart, it was Ringwood's premier coaching inn throughout the 19th century. Note the elaborate bracket and lamp over the door, now sadly missing.

Turning left into Southampton Road, the road immediately narrows once more. Early in the 20th century, this was known as Southampton Street or Up Street. Of all the roads in Ringwood other than the A31, Southampton Road has changed the most over the last hundred years. In the early 1900s it was a very important road as all the traffic to and from Southampton, Winchester and London would have passed along it. The road was lined with a jumble of small brick Victorian terraced houses, mixed in with a collection of older Georgian properties.

Every single one of the buildings on the left side of photograph 65632 (pages 74-75) has since been demolished and replaced by modern shops. F W Woolworth was the first to be built about 1937, and originally its ground floor extended out in line with the old existing buildings. Soon afterwards a parade of shops was erected adjoining Woolworths. At the

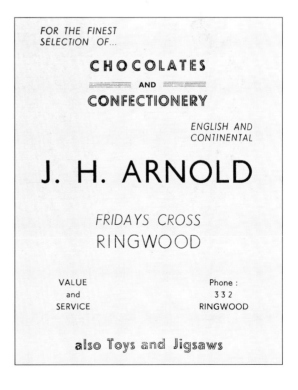

**Southampton Street
1913** 65632

It is noticeable that all the properties on the left-hand side appear to be private houses, although trades were being carried out from many of them. Later in the century, shop fronts were inserted. For example, the house directly behind the two girls became W T Thorner, boot-maker and wool shop, quite an unusual combination! On the right-hand side is the shop of Mr James Gardener the printer, later taken over by Brown & Son. Next door is the Post Office, which had recently relocated from the High Street to this new purpose-built office (now the Job Centre). On the extreme right is Mr Morgan the tailor. Note the lamps over his shop actually fitted through the blind.

same time the opportunity was taken to set the new shops further back so that the road could be widened at a future date. However, by the time the old houses nearer Fridays Cross were redeveloped in the 1970s, policy had changed and the new shops were built closer to the original street frontage. This has left part of Southampton Road with the widest pavement in town. More changes occurred further up the road when Monmouth Court was built and White's garage was demolished to make way for Gateway supermarket (now Somerfield) in the 1970s.

Soon afterwards Southampton Road was altered dramatically when Mansfield Road was constructed. What had once been the main road to Southampton across the New Forest now had to suffer the indignity of being cut in half by a new feeder road to the ever busier A31. Although all these changes in planning have left Southampton Road with a rather hotchpotch confusion of poor architecture and variable pavement widths, the road between Fridays Cross and the Mansfield Road crossing is still a busy shopping place, containing many of Ringwood's most popular shops.

Right: Southampton Road c1950 R35022

The advertisement for Strong's of Romsey beer, on the side of Tanners the builders, reminded motorists that they were 'In the heart of the Strong Country'. Nowadays local beer is brewed by Ringwood Brewery in Christchurch Road. The location of the billboard is more appropriate than was probably realised at the time, because in the early 19th century this was once the Compton Arms public house. The single-storey shop adjoining Tanners was used by the Women's Institute Market. These buildings were demolished in the 1960s and replaced by the block containing Wilkins the bakers (now Blockbuster Video). On the other side of the road White's garage, otherwise known as Ringwood Motor Works, sold and serviced cars from 1923-1970.

Right: Southampton Road c1950 R35018

Southampton Road today contains many of Ringwood's popular multiples, including two dispensing chemists, Boots and Lloyds, and Superdrug. Fifty years ago the local chemists were W S Stephenson Ltd, seen to the right of F W Woolworth in this photograph, Randall & Wilson at Fridays Cross, and P C Cartledge and W E Kirkman in the High Street.

The Congregational Chapel 1890 24060

The three buildings seen to the left of the chapel have all been demolished. The corner shop, with the man and boy standing outside, belonged to George Wiseman, grocer and greengrocer. Where the shed stands, on the right of the chapel, is now the entrance to Woodstock Lane.

In 1892 the rear of the house on the right (now Streets Toyshop) became the first premises of Davis Garage. Originally entitled Davis Cycle Works, the business was founded to make and sell cycles, sewing machines and perambulators. With the coming of the car and motorcycle the business started to cater for the motorist. In 1916 the Davis family moved to the Dyer's house in the High Street and turned it into a garage.

The road leading south from Fridays Cross was originally known as Christchurch Street. Unfortunately there are no Frith photographs of the stretch of this road between Fridays Cross and the Congregational Chapel, now Trinity United Reformed Church.

The Frith photographs in this part of the collection are mainly early ones. The picture of the Congregational Chapel (24060) was taken in 1890, thirty years before the War Memorial was erected. A row of elm trees can be seen where the memorial now stands. There was of course no mini-roundabout or Mansfield Road in those days.

The Congregational Chapel was built in 1865 at a cost of £6000. The architect was H T Helyer of Ryde, Isle of Wight. It was built of white brick and Bath stone dressings, with two spires 65 feet high. The church is not much altered today, other than the absence of its imposing railings and pillared gateway.

Non-conformism has always been strong in Ringwood, with roots right back to the turbulent 17th century. Soldiers broke up an early meeting of Quakers at Merryweather Farm in 1663 and Dame Alice Lisle was arrested for sheltering a Presbyterian minister during the Monmouth Rebellion of 1685. This act led to her trial by the infamous Judge Jefferies and her subsequent execution at Winchester. During the 18th century a new atmosphere of religious toleration enabled both the Presbyterians (later Unitarians) and the Independents (later Congregationalists) to establish Meeting Houses in Ringwood. Baptists and Methodists also set up their own chapels in Ringwood during the 19th century.

The more southerly part of Christchurch Road is probably the least altered of all the main streets of old Ringwood. Arthur Kingsbury in his 'History of Ringwood' wrote in 1894, 'Here the street has been recently widened, and a row of new villa residences built on an old nursery ground on the one side, stand in strong contrast with the medley of old houses on the other.' The three late Victorian villas still look much as they did a hundred years ago, except that their gates and iron railings have gone and their porches altered. A fourth house was demolished to build the Fire Station.

Similarly, the railings in front of Netherbrook House and St Katharine's have also disappeared but the thatched cottages, one still retaining its high front doorstep, remain. The only obvious change has been

Christchurch Street 1900 45033

the demolition of the very old timbered cottages shown in photograph 45033 (page 81). These were demolished in the 1920s and replaced by a furniture shop, built by Charlie Britten, and remembered by many as Rowbothams. This shop, with its stained glass window tops and its cast iron column, was itself demolished in 2001 to the great indignation of Ringwood townsfolk.

Back on the opposite side of the road, Crescent House and the thatched house next to it are still easily recognisable. Neither has The Lamb Inn altered a great deal over the past hundred years. Note the sign to the Railway Station painted on the side of the Lamb wall in photograph 45035.

Although it has been envisaged that this journey through Ringwood began with an imaginary traveller arriving by road from the west, it is more than likely that Frith's early photographer arrived and departed from the town by railway. It is therefore appropriate to end the book at the south end of town, nearest the Railway Station. What a pity that the photographer omitted to take a picture of the station while he was about it!

As Mr Kingsbury explained in his book of 1894, 'the first turning on the left, up Lamb Lane [now Hightown Road], leads to the Railway station, which is large and commodious considering the size of the town. It narrowly escaped being the chief junction for Bournemouth, for the Railway Company was thinking about doubling the local branch, but its corporate mind was so long coming to a decision, during which Bournemouth grew so rapidly that it was finally decided to construct a more direct line from Brockenhurst.' The railway finally closed in 1964 under the Beeching cuts.

The two photographs of Coxstone Lane, leading from Christchurch Road to the

Above: **Christchurch Street 1900** 45034

One of the Victorian villas shown in this image (which is looking the other way from 45033), then appropriately named Balaclava, was the home of local hero Captain James Hefferon (1835-1909). As a young man he rode in the famous cavalry Charge of the Light Brigade as a trumpeter. He survived this ill-fated mission and went on to serve in the 8th King's Royal Hussars throughout the rest of the Crimean War, the Indian Mutiny and the Afghan War. When he died in 1909 he was given a military funeral that solemnly processed from his house to the Parish Church and ended with rifles fired over his grave in the cemetery.

Right: **Christchurch Street 1900** 45035

Coxstone Lane 1913
65639

The cart with a pile of sacks on it may have belonged to Charlie Palmer, who had a hardware shop on the corner of Coxstone Lane. Sadly this cottage (by then Greenfields butchery shop) and the adjoining row in Christchurch Road were burnt down in 1959 when a spark from a passing goods train caught light to the thatch of the cottage nearest the railway line.

Bickerley, end the collection with typical Frith pictures of 'chocolate box' thatched cottages. These cottages, like the Old Cottage in West Street, have remained relatively unchanged over the past century.

To celebrate the Millennium, the Ringwood Camera Club took a number of photographs to record Ringwood in the year 2000. Pictures of Coxstone Lane were once again a popular choice. These photographs have now been deposited in a time capsule buried in the Market Place. If at the end of the 21st century the capsule is re-opened, we hope the future residents of Ringwood will still be able to recognise and appreciate the captured images.

It is hoped that in the same way the reader will want to keep this record of Frith photographs of Ringwood as a memento of a much-loved town.

Coxstone Lane c1955 R35046

Thatched cottages have always been a favourite subject of photographers. Today it is still common to see visitors writing a postcard picturing the thatched cottages of Ringwood, just as they did a hundred years ago. This has always been the favourite sort of picture visitors to Ringwood want to buy, either to keep for themselves as a memento or to send to their friends.

Index

Frith Book Co Titles

www.francisfrith.co.uk

The Frith Book Company publishes over 100 new titles each year. A selection of those currently available are listed below. For latest catalogue please contact Frith Book Co.

Town Books 96 pages, approx 100 photos. County and Themed Books 128 pages, approx 150 photos (unless specified). All titles hardback laminated case and jacket except those indicated pb (paperback).

Amersham, Chesham & Rickmansworth (pb)	1-85937-340-2	£9.99
Ancient Monuments & Stone Circles	1-85937-143-4	£17.99
Aylesbury (pb)	1-85937-227-9	£9.99
Bakewell	1-85937-113-2	£12.99
Barnstaple (pb)	1-85937-300-3	£9.99
Bath (pb)	1-85937419-0	£9.99
Bedford (pb)	1-85937-205-8	£9.99
Berkshire (pb)	1-85937-191-4	£9.99
Berkshire Churches	1-85937-170-1	£17.99
Blackpool (pb)	1-85937-382-8	£9.99
Bognor Regis (pb)	1-85937-431-x	£9.99
Bournemouth	1-85937-067-5	£12.99
Bradford (pb)	1-85937-204-x	£9.99
Brighton & Hove(pb)	1-85937-192-2	£8.99
Bristol (pb)	1-85937-264-3	£9.99
British Life A Century Ago (pb)	1-85937-213-9	£9.99
Buckinghamshire (pb)	1-85937-200-7	£9.99
Camberley (pb)	1-85937-222-8	£9.99
Cambridge (pb)	1-85937-422-0	£9.99
Cambridgeshire (pb)	1-85937-420-4	£9.99
Canals & Waterways (pb)	1-85937-291-0	£9.99
Canterbury Cathedral (pb)	1-85937-179-5	£9.99
Cardiff (pb)	1-85937-093-4	£9.99
Carmarthenshire	1-85937-216-3	£14.99
Chelmsford (pb)	1-85937-310-0	£9.99
Cheltenham (pb)	1-85937-095-0	£9.99
Cheshire (pb)	1-85937-271-6	£9.99
Chester	1-85937-090-x	£12.99
Chesterfield	1-85937-378-x	£9.99
Chichester (pb)	1-85937-228-7	£9.99
Colchester (pb)	1-85937-188-4	£8.99
Cornish Coast	1-85937-163-9	£14.99
Cornwall (pb)	1-85937-229-5	£9.99
Cornwall Living Memories	1-85937-248-1	£14.99
Cotswolds (pb)	1-85937-230-9	£9.99
Cotswolds Living Memories	1-85937-255-4	£14.99
County Durham	1-85937-123-x	£14.99
Croydon Living Memories	1-85937-162-0	£9.99
Cumbria	1-85937-101-9	£14.99
Dartmoor	1-85937-145-0	£14.99
Derby (pb)	1-85937-367-4	£9.99
Derbyshire (pb)	1-85937-196-5	£9.99
Devon (pb)	1-85937-297-x	£9.99
Dorset (pb)	1-85937-269-4	£9.99
Dorset Churches	1-85937-172-8	£17.99
Dorset Coast (pb)	1-85937-299-6	£9.99
Dorset Living Memories	1-85937-210-4	£14.99
Down the Severn	1-85937-118-3	£14.99
Down the Thames (pb)	1-85937-278-3	£9.99
Down the Trent	1-85937-311-9	£14.99
Dublin (pb)	1-85937-231-7	£9.99
East Anglia (pb)	1-85937-265-1	£9.99
East London	1-85937-080-2	£14.99
East Sussex	1-85937-130-2	£14.99
Eastbourne	1-85937-061-6	£12.99
Edinburgh (pb)	1-85937-193-0	£8.99
England in the 1880s	1-85937-331-3	£17.99
English Castles (pb)	1-85937-434-4	£9.99
English Country Houses	1-85937-161-2	£17.99
Essex (pb)	1-85937-270-8	£9.99
Exeter	1-85937-126-4	£12.99
Exmoor	1-85937-132-9	£14.99
Falmouth	1-85937-066-7	£12.99
Folkestone (pb)	1-85937-124-8	£9.99
Glasgow (pb)	1-85937-190-6	£9.99
Gloucestershire	1-85937-102-7	£14.99
Great Yarmouth (pb)	1-85937-426-3	£9.99
Greater Manchester (pb)	1-85937-266-x	£9.99
Guildford (pb)	1-85937-410-7	£9.99
Hampshire (pb)	1-85937-279-1	£9.99
Hampshire Churches (pb)	1-85937-207-4	£9.99
Harrogate	1-85937-423-9	£9.99
Hastings & Bexhill (pb)	1-85937-131-0	£9.99
Heart of Lancashire (pb)	1-85937-197-3	£9.99
Helston (pb)	1-85937-214-7	£9.99
Hereford (pb)	1-85937-175-2	£9.99
Herefordshire	1-85937-174-4	£14.99
Hertfordshire (pb)	1-85937-247-3	£9.99
Horsham (pb)	1-85937-432-8	£9.99
Humberside	1-85937-215-5	£14.99
Hythe, Romney Marsh & Ashford	1-85937-256-2	£9.99

Available from your local bookshop or from the publisher

Frith Book Co Titles (continued)

Ipswich (pb)	1-85937-424-7	£9.99	St Ives (pb)	1-85937415-8	£9.99
Ireland (pb)	1-85937-181-7	£9.99	Scotland (pb)	1-85937-182-5	£9.99
Isle of Man (pb)	1-85937-268-6	£9.99	Scottish Castles (pb)	1-85937-323-2	£9.99
Isles of Scilly	1-85937-136-1	£14.99	Sevenoaks & Tunbridge	1-85937-057-8	£12.99
Isle of Wight (pb)	1-85937-429-8	£9.99	Sheffield, South Yorks (pb)	1-85937-267-8	£9.99
Isle of Wight Living Memories	1-85937-304-6	£14.99	Shrewsbury (pb)	1-85937-325-9	£9.99
Kent (pb)	1-85937-189-2	£9.99	Shropshire (pb)	1-85937-326-7	£9.99
Kent Living Memories	1-85937-125-6	£14.99	Somerset	1-85937-153-1	£14.99
Lake District (pb)	1-85937-275-9	£9.99	South Devon Coast	1-85937-107-8	£14.99
Lancaster, Morecambe & Heysham (pb)	1-85937-233-3	£9.99	South Devon Living Memories	1-85937-168-x	£14.99
Leeds (pb)	1-85937-202-3	£9.99	South Hams	1-85937-220-1	£14.99
Leicester	1-85937-073-x	£12.99	Southampton (pb)	1-85937-427-1	£9.99
Leicestershire (pb)	1-85937-185-x	£9.99	Southport (pb)	1-85937-425-5	£9.99
Lincolnshire (pb)	1-85937-433-6	£9.99	Staffordshire	1-85937-047-0	£12.99
Liverpool & Merseyside (pb)	1-85937-234-1	£9.99	Stratford upon Avon	1-85937-098-5	£12.99
London (pb)	1-85937-183-3	£9.99	Suffolk (pb)	1-85937-221-x	£9.99
Ludlow (pb)	1-85937-176-0	£9.99	Suffolk Coast	1-85937-259-7	£14.99
Luton (pb)	1-85937-235-x	£9.99	Surrey (pb)	1-85937-240-6	£9.99
Maidstone	1-85937-056-x	£14.99	Sussex (pb)	1-85937-184-1	£9.99
Manchester (pb)	1-85937-198-1	£9.99	Swansea (pb)	1-85937-167-1	£9.99
Middlesex	1-85937-158-2	£14.99	Tees Valley & Cleveland	1-85937-211-2	£14.99
New Forest	1-85937-128-0	£14.99	Thanet (pb)	1-85937-116-7	£9.99
Newark (pb)	1-85937-366-6	£9.99	Tiverton (pb)	1-85937-178-7	£9.99
Newport, Wales (pb)	1-85937-258-9	£9.99	Torbay	1-85937-063-2	£12.99
Newquay (pb)	1-85937-421-2	£9.99	Truro	1-85937-147-7	£12.99
Norfolk (pb)	1-85937-195-7	£9.99	Victorian and Edwardian Cornwall	1-85937-252-x	£14.99
Norfolk Living Memories	1-85937-217-1	£14.99	Victorian & Edwardian Devon	1-85937-253-8	£14.99
Northamptonshire	1-85937-150-7	£14.99	Victorian & Edwardian Kent	1-85937-149-3	£14.99
Northumberland Tyne & Wear (pb)	1-85937-281-3	£9.99	Vic & Ed Maritime Album	1-85937-144-2	£17.99
North Devon Coast	1-85937-146-9	£14.99	Victorian and Edwardian Sussex	1-85937-157-4	£14.99
North Devon Living Memories	1-85937-261-9	£14.99	Victorian & Edwardian Yorkshire	1-85937-154-x	£14.99
North London	1-85937-206-6	£14.99	Victorian Seaside	1-85937-159-0	£17.99
North Wales (pb)	1-85937-298-8	£9.99	Villages of Devon (pb)	1-85937-293-7	£9.99
North Yorkshire (pb)	1-85937-236-8	£9.99	Villages of Kent (pb)	1-85937-294-5	£9.99
Norwich (pb)	1-85937-194-9	£8.99	Villages of Sussex (pb)	1-85937-295-3	£9.99
Nottingham (pb)	1-85937-324-0	£9.99	Warwickshire (pb)	1-85937-203-1	£9.99
Nottinghamshire (pb)	1-85937-187-6	£9.99	Welsh Castles (pb)	1-85937-322-4	£9.99
Oxford (pb)	1-85937-411-5	£9.99	West Midlands (pb)	1-85937-289-9	£9.99
Oxfordshire (pb)	1-85937-430-1	£9.99	West Sussex	1-85937-148-5	£14.99
Peak District (pb)	1-85937-280-5	£9.99	West Yorkshire (pb)	1-85937-201-5	£9.99
Penzance	1-85937-069-1	£12.99	Weymouth (pb)	1-85937-209-0	£9.99
Peterborough (pb)	1-85937-219-8	£9.99	Wiltshire (pb)	1-85937-277-5	£9.99
Piers	1-85937-237-6	£17.99	Wiltshire Churches (pb)	1-85937-171-x	£9.99
Plymouth	1-85937-119-1	£12.99	Wiltshire Living Memories	1-85937-245-7	£14.99
Poole & Sandbanks (pb)	1-85937-251-1	£9.99	Winchester (pb)	1-85937-428-x	£9.99
Preston (pb)	1-85937-212-0	£9.99	Windmills & Watermills	1-85937-242-2	£17.99
Reading (pb)	1-85937-238-4	£9.99	Worcester (pb)	1-85937-165-5	£9.99
Romford (pb)	1-85937-319-4	£9.99	Worcestershire	1-85937-152-3	£14.99
Salisbury (pb)	1-85937-239-2	£9.99	York (pb)	1-85937-199-x	£9.99
Scarborough (pb)	1-85937-379-8	£9.99	Yorkshire (pb)	1-85937-186-8	£9.99
St Albans (pb)	1-85937-341-0	£9.99	Yorkshire Living Memories	1-85937-166-3	£14.99

See Frith books on the internet www.francisfrith.co.uk

FRITH PRODUCTS & SERVICES

Francis Frith would doubtless be pleased to know that the pioneering publishing venture he started in 1860 still continues today. A hundred and forty years later, The Francis Frith Collection continues in the same innovative tradition and is now one of the foremost publishers of vintage photographs in the world. Some of the current activities include:

Interior Decoration

Today Frith's photographs can be seen framed and as giant wall murals in thousands of pubs, restaurants, hotels, banks, retail stores and other public buildings throughout the country. In every case they enhance the unique local atmosphere of the places they depict and provide reminders of gentler days in an increasingly busy and frenetic world.

Product Promotions

Frith products are used by many major companies to promote the sales of their own products or to reinforce their own history and heritage. Frith promotions have been used by Hovis bread, Courage beers, Scots Porage Oats, Colman's mustard, Cadbury's foods, Mellow Birds coffee, Dunhill pipe tobacco, Guinness, and Bulmer's Cider.

Genealogy and Family History

As the interest in family history and roots grows world-wide, more and more people are turning to Frith's photographs of Great Britain for images of the towns, villages and streets where their ancestors lived; and, of course, photographs of the churches and chapels where their ancestors were christened, married and buried are an essential part of every genealogy tree and family album.

Frith Products

All Frith photographs are available Framed or just as Mounted Prints and Posters (size 23 x 16 inches). These may be ordered from the address below. From time to time other products - Address Books, Calendars, Table Mats, etc - are available.

The Internet

Already twenty thousand Frith photographs can be viewed and purchased on the internet through the Frith websites and a myriad of partner sites.

For more detailed information on Frith companies and products, look at these sites:

www.francisfrith.co.uk
www.francisfrith.com
(for North American visitors)

See the complete list of Frith Books at:

www.francisfrith.co.uk

This web site is regularly updated with the latest list of publications from the Frith Book Company. If you wish to buy books relating to another part of the country that your local bookshop does not stock, you may purchase on-line.

For further information, trade, or author enquiries please contact us at the address below:
The Francis Frith Collection, Frith's Barn, Teffont, Salisbury, Wiltshire, England SP3 5QP.
Tel: +44 (0)1722 716 376 Fax: +44 (0)1722 716 881 Email: sales@francisfrith.co.uk

See Frith books on the internet www.francisfrith.co.uk

TO RECEIVE YOUR FREE MOUNTED PRINT

Mounted Print
Overall size 14 x 11 inches

Cut out this Voucher and return it with your remittance for £1.95 to cover postage and handling, to UK addresses. For overseas addresses please include £4.00 post and handling. Choose any photograph included in this book. Your SEPIA print will be A4 in size, and mounted in a cream mount with burgundy rule line, overall size 14 x 11 inches.

Order additional Mounted Prints at HALF PRICE (only £7.49 each*)

If there are further pictures you would like to order, possibly as gifts for friends and family, purchase them at half price (no additional postage and handling required).

Have your Mounted Prints framed*

For an additional £14.95 per print you can have your chosen Mounted Print framed in an elegant polished wood and gilt moulding, overall size 16 x 13 inches (no additional postage and handling required).

---

* IMPORTANT!
These special prices are only available if ordered using the original voucher on this page (no copies permitted) and at the same time as your free Mounted Print, for delivery to the same address

---

Frith Collectors' Guild

From time to time we publish a magazine of news and stories about Frith photographs and further special offers of Frith products. If you would like 12 months FREE membership, please return this form.

Send completed forms to:
The Francis Frith Collection, Frith's Barn, Teffont, Salisbury, Wiltshire SP3 5QP

Voucher for FREE and Reduced Price Frith Prints

Picture no.	Page number	Qty	Mounted @ £7.49	Framed + £14.95	Total Cost
		1	**Free of charge***	£	£
			£7.49	£	£
			£7.49	£	£
			£7.49	£	£
			£7.49	£	£
			£7.49	£	£

Please allow 28 days for delivery	*** Post & handling** £1.95
Book Title	**Total Order Cost** £

Please do not photocopy this voucher. Only the original is valid, so please cut it out and return it to us.

I enclose a cheque / postal order for £ . . . . made payable to 'The Francis Frith Collection'
OR please debit my Mastercard / Visa / Switch / Amex card
(credit cards please on all overseas orders)

Number . . . .

Issue No (Switch only) . . . . .Valid from (Amex/Switch) . . . .

Expires . . . . Signature . . . .

Name Mr/Mrs/Ms . . . .

Address . . . .

. . . .

. . . .

. . . . Postcode . . . .

Daytime Tel No . . . . Valid to 31/12/02

The Francis Frith Collectors' Guild

Please enrol me as a member for 12 months free of charge.

Name Mr/Mrs/Ms . . . .

Address . . . .

. . . .

. . . .

. . . . Postcode . . . .

Would you like to find out more about Francis Frith?

We have recently recruited some entertaining speakers who are happy to visit local groups, clubs and societies to give an illustrated talk documenting Frith's travels and photographs. If you are a member of such a group and are interested in hosting a presentation, we would love to hear from you.

Our speakers bring with them a small selection of our local town and county books, together with sample prints. They are happy to take orders. A small proportion of the order value is donated to the group who have hosted the presentation. The talks are therefore an excellent way of fundraising for small groups and societies.

Can you help us with information about any of the Frith photographs in this book?

We are gradually compiling an historical record for each of the photographs in the Frith archive. It is always fascinating to find out the names of the people shown in the pictures, as well as insights into the shops, buildings and other features depicted.

If you recognize anyone in the photographs in this book, or if you have information not already included in the author's caption, do let us know. We would love to hear from you, and will try to publish it in future books or articles.

Our production team

Frith books are produced by a small dedicated team at offices in the converted Grade II listed 18th-century barn at Teffont near Salisbury, illustrated above. Most have worked with the Frith Collection for many years. All have in common one quality: they have a passion for the Frith Collection. The team is constantly expanding, but currently includes:

Jason Buck, John Buck, Douglas Burns, Heather Crisp, Isobel Hall, Rob Hames, Hazel Heaton, Peter Horne, James Kinnear, Tina Leary, Hannah Marsh, Eliza Sackett, Terence Sackett, Sandra Sanger, Shelley Tolcher, Susanna Walker, Clive Wathen and Jenny Wathen.

Free Print - see overleaf